IRISH

AND

MARRIAGE JOKES

by

Des MacHale

THE MERCIER PRESS
Cork and Dublin

The Mercier Press, 4 Bridge Street, Cork.
24 Lower Abbey Street, Dublin 1.

ISBN O 85342 500 O

Printed by the Leinster Leader Ltd., Naas, Co. Kildare.

INTRODUCTION

Ireland has the unenviable record of having the highest average age for marriage in the world. The average Irishman does not marry until he is over 31, while the average Irishwoman does not marry until she is over 26. On the other hand, Irish families tend to be large and it is not uncommon to find fathers up to fifty years older than their children. These facts could possibly be explained by a complex combination of factors drawn from Sociology, Religion, History, and Economics, but that is not the function of this little book.

Irish attitudes to love and marriage are slowly changing. The average age for marriage in both men and women is slowly decreasing, possibly because of industrialisation and the greater economic independence of young people. Family size too is decreasing, perhaps because of changing attitudes to reproduction and the economics of rearing a large number of children.

A period of transition almost inevitably gives rise to insecurity and a natural way to dispel the resultant anxiety is to laugh and joke about our earlier attitudes towards love and marriage. Not surprisingly, this book smacks of male chauvinist piggery rather than female chauvinist sowery, because the Irish male cannot feel very proud of his treatment of the Irish female over the last few thousand years. On the other hand, the Irish female is probably just as culpable because of the way in which she spoiled her sons and reared them to be anything but good husband material.

The battle of the sexes continues, in Ireland as everywhere else, but let us take a break from the battle and sit back and laugh about it a little. I have tried to keep this collection as inoffensive as possible because basically I believe that jokes should be heard and not obscene. I have recorded some of the comments of great Irish writers on the subjects of love and marriage. All of these writers are male. Irishwomen, being much more sensible than Irishmen, have kept their mouths shut on the subject.

Finally, a word about my hero and heroine, Pat and Bridget. Pat is the eternal bachelor, the reluctant husband, the embarrassed father, and the lonely widower. Bridget is the hopeful spinster, the long-suffering wife, the proud mother, and the relieved widow. I am sentimental enough to believe that beneath all the trouble and strife that occurs between them, there lurks a little affection and respect, and dare I say it, love.

Pat and Bridget are real and any resemblance between them and any Irishman and Irishwoman living or dead is quite deliberate.

TO MY PARENTS
THE HAPPIEST OF MARRIAGES

What do you call an Irishman who knows how to control a wife?
A bachelor.

****

A witness was giving evidence at a court case where Pat was accused of mistreating his wife Bridget.
Judge: 'Were you present at the beginning of the trouble between Pat and Bridget?'
Witness: 'Sure I was — wasn't I the best man at their wedding.'

****

Pat and Bridget had been courting for over twenty years but Pat was still a little shy, so one cold night Bridget decided to encourage him a little.
'Pat,' she said, 'when I was a little girl my mother used to put her arms around me to keep me warm on cold nights.'
'Surely,' said Pat, 'you don't expect me to go all the way back for your mother at this hour of the night?'

****

An Irishman has been defined as somebody who would trample over twelve naked women to reach a bottle of Guinness.

****

Pat was five feet tall while Bridget was six foot three, but some fellows will go to any lengths. One night when they were walking by the old forge he asked for a kiss and Bridget consented. So he stood on an old anvil and gave her a little kiss. They walked on and after a few miles he asked her for another kiss.
'No,' she replied haughtily, 'I've given you all the kisses you're going to get for tonight.'
'In that case,' said Pat in disgust, 'I'm not going to carry this anvil one step further.'

****

'My wife eloped with my best friend,' a fellow told Pat.
'What was his name?' asked Pat.
'I don't know,' said the fellow, 'I never met him.'

Pat was helping at Bridget's first confinement by holding the oil lamp. When Bridget had produced a son, a daughter and another son in quick succession, Pat suddenly put the lamp out.

'Relight that lamp at once,' said the midwife, 'I think there's another.'

'I will not,' said Pat, 'it's the light that's attracting them.'

****

A harmless little film was doing the rounds of country villages. One particular sequence showed a shapely young lady changing her clothes, but just as the scene was becoming exciting, a very long train came into view obscuring the lady. By the time the train had passed she was fully dressed again.

Pat followed the film from one town to another until he must have seen it at least twenty times. 'I'm not as daft as I seem,' he explained, 'some night that train is going to be late.'

****

'A man can be happy with any woman as long as he does not love her.'

Oscar Wilde.

****

Pat and Bridget had seventeen children so the Vatican decided to present them with a gold medal struck specially in their honour. The Papal Nuncio delivered the medal in person and told them that they were a credit to the Catholic Church.

'There must be some mistake,' said Pat, 'we're Protestants.'

'Oh my God,' said the Papal Nuncio, 'don't tell me we've minted a gold medal for two sex-crazy Protestants.'

****

'Phone the doctor yourself woman,' said Pat to his wife Bridget, 'you're doing nothing else between contractions.'

6

After a twenty year courtship Pat proposed to Bridget and was accepted, so he went to her father to ask his permission.

'I've been courting your daughter for twenty years sir,' he said shyly.

'And what do you want now?' Bridget's father asked.

'Her hand in marriage sir,' said Pat.

'Thank goodness,' her father replied, 'for a moment I thought you wanted a pension.'

****

'Bridget, we've been courting in this field now for ten years,' said Pat one night.

'That's right,' said Bridget nostalgically.

'Well, we won't be courting here this time next year,' said Pat.

'Why is that Pat?' asked Bridget hopefully.

'Because the County Council have just bought it for house building.'

****

Definition of an Irish queer — a fellow who prefers women to drink.

****

After a whirlwind five year courtship Pat decided to pop the question:

'Bridget,' he said, 'how would you like to put your shoes under my bed?'

'Whatever can you mean Pat?' said Bridget blushingly.

'What I really mean,' said Pat, 'is, how would you like to be buried with my people?'

****

I wish that Adam had died with all his ribs in his body.

Dion Boucicault.

****

'The ideal wife,' said Pat, 'should be like a bank note. At forty you should be able to swop her for two twenties.'

Pat and Bridget were courting in a dark corner when they were disturbed by a policeman with a torch.

'What are you doing in there?' the policeman asked.

'Nothing,' said Pat.

'Well hold this torch,' said the policeman, 'and let me in there.'

****

Pat was very ill indeed so Bridget sent for the doctor. After a brief examination the doctor announced that Pat was dead.

'I'm not,' said Pat feebly from his bed.

'Be quiet,' said Bridget, 'do you know better than the doctor?'

****

Pat was being introduced to Bridget on the night before their wedding. Seeing that she was lame, over fifteen stone, and had only one eye, Pat took his father into the next room to complain.

'I couldn't possibly marry her,' he whispered, 'she's not at all suitable.'

'You don't have to whisper,' said his father, 'she's deaf too.'

****

After a period of about six months of widowhood Bridget again decided to enter the married state. Some weeks after she remarried an old friend met her in the street dressed in the deepest mourning.

'Why Bridget,' she asked, 'for whom are you in mourning?'

'For Pat,' answered Bridget, 'my first husband. When he died I was that poor I couldn't afford to buy mourning clothes, but I said if ever I could I would, and my new husband Jim is as generous as a lord.'

****

Pat: 'The very next time you contradict me I'm going to kiss you.

Bridget: 'You will not.'

****

Bridget: 'This is our tenth wedding anniversary. Let's have a chicken from our own farm for dinner to celebrate.'

Pat: 'Why kill an innocent bird for what happened ten years ago?'

****

Pat was phoning the doctor.
'Doctor', he said, 'my wife Bridget dislocated her jaw last night and hasn't spoken for nearly ten hours. If you happen to be in the neighbourhood sometime this month maybe you could drop in and have a look at her.'

****

Pat and Bridget were going on vacation in their motor-car and Bridget was sitting in the back seat. A policeman flagged Pat down and told him that they had just received a telephone call informing them that Bridget had fallen out of the car and had been found on the roadside about thirty miles back.
'Thank goodness,' said Pat, 'I thought I'd gone deaf.'

****

Pat, who was an eligible bachelor, visited Bridget, an elderly widow in his district every evening and had tea with her. A friend suggested that he should marry her.
'I have often thought about it,' said Pat, 'but where would I spend my evenings then?'

****

'Have you a big family?' Bridget was once asked.
'Eight,' she replied, 'five by the second wife of my third husband and three by the third wife of my first.'

****

'Are you any relation of Mick's?' Pat was asked.
'A distant relative,' he replied, 'I was my mother's first child and he was the thirteenth.'

****

Pat, a farmhand, went off courting Bridget one evening carrying a lantern. He was met by the farmer who complained about the fact that he was using his lantern containing his oil.

'I never had a lantern when I went courting,' he continued.

'If you had,' retorted Pat, 'you might have married a better-looking wife.'

****

'Pat, do you love me?' Bridget asked.
'Yes,' said Pat.
'Do you think I'm beautiful?'
'Yes,' said Pat.
'Is my figure divine?'
'Yes,' said Pat.
'Are my eyes like diamonds?'
'Yes,' said Pat.
'Oh Pat, you say the nicest things,' said Bridget, 'say some more.'

****

Bridget awoke one night screaming with pain, so Pat phoned the doctor.

'Come quickly,' he told him, 'my wife Bridget is in pain—I think it's her appendix.'

'Go back to bed,' the doctor told him, 'I took out your wife's appendix over four years ago and I never heard of anyone having another appendix!.

'Did you ever hear of anybody having another wife?' asked Pat.

****

Men always want to be a woman's first love —
Women always want to be a man's last romance.

Oscar Wilde.

****

Bridget finally married Pat who was an X—ray specialist.
He was the only one who could ever see anything in her.

****

Bridget was expecting her first baby.
'Do you ever get a craving for strange exotic food?' a friend asked her.
'I do,' said Bridget.
'Like what?' asked the friend.
'Wedding cake,' said Bridget.

****

Pat's brother Mick was lucky in love — he's still a bachelor.

****

Pat was a bit shy so when Bridget had thrown her arms around him and kissed him for bringing her a bunch of flowers he got up and started to leave.
'I'm sorry if I offended you,' said Bridget.
'Oh, I'm not offended,' replied Pat, 'I'm going for more flowers.'

****

Bridget: 'What's on your mind Pat?'
Pat: 'I'm just wondering if my father would look after the farm while were on our honeymoon, supposing you said "yes" if I asked you to marry me.'

****

Bridget went into the city store to pay the final instalment on her pram.
'And how is the baby?' asked the clerk.
'I'm fine thanks,' said Bridget.

****

Three things that are as good as other things —
        Dirty water to quench a fire;
        A bad suit of clothes on a drunkard;
        A blind man's ugly wife.

                                        Old Irish Proverb.

'Do you know Tom McCarthy?' Pat was asked.
'Know him? ' cried Pat, 'why he's a near relation. He once proposed to a sister of mine.'

****

Bridget and her friend were returning from the annual mission
where the priest had just preached a sermon on married life.
'What did you think of the sermon?' the friend asked.
'I wish,' said Bridget, 'that I knew as little about it as he did.'

****

Bridget died and only a month later Pat announced his plans
to remarry.
'But your wife is dead only a month,' his mother protested.
'She's as dead now as she'll ever be,' said Pat.

****

Sir John Mahaffy, one of Oscar Wilde's instructors at Trinity
College was once asked by a student what, in his opinion, was
the principal difference between men and women.
'I can't conceive,' retorted Mahaffy.

****

*Long engagements give people the opportunity of finding out
each other's character before marriage, which is never advisable.*

Oscar Wilde.

****

Priest (writing a certificate at the baptismal ceremony and
trying to remember the date): 'Let me see, is this the nine-
teenth?
Bridget: 'Indeed it's not, it is only our thirteenth.'

****

Pat and Bridget were walking home one dark night. 'Oh Pat, I'm so afraid,' said Bridget. 'And what are you afraid of, girl?' said Pat. 'I'm afraid you might be going to kiss me.' 'Sure how could I kiss you girl, with a goose under one arm and a tub under the other?' 'Oh Pat, I'm afraid that you might put the goose on the ground, put the tub on top of her, sit down on the tub, take me in your arms, and then kiss me.'

****

Pat and Bridget were being examined by the parish priest as to their fitness to enter the married state. 'And what,' he asked them, 'is the best preparation for the sacrament of matrimony?' 'A little courting, father,' replied Pat and Bridget simultaneously.

****

'It's a great pleasure to be alone,' reflected Pat, 'especially when Bridget is with me.'

****

PAT'S LOVE LETTER TO BRIDGET

My Darling Bridget,
			I met you last night and you never came. Next time I'll meet you again whether you come or not. If I am there first, I'll write my name on the gatepost to let you know; and if it's you that's first, rub out my name and nobody will be any the wiser.
			Darling Bridget, I would climb the highest mountain for your sake, and swim the widest sea. I would endure any hardships and suffer any trial to spend a moment by your side.

Your own ever loving
Pat.

P.S. I'll be over to see you on Friday night if it's not raining.

****

Bridget's younger sister Mary rushed home and told her mother that she was about to be married in the morning.

'To whom, for God's sake?' her mother asked in alarm.

'To one of the O'Flaherty boys,' replied Mary shyly.

'Which one of them?'

'Well,' said Mary, 'it was rather dark in the corner near the fireplace where he proposed, and I don't rightly know which one of the O'Flaherty's it was.'

****

Pat and Bridget were penniless so when they went to be married they were in a fix when the priest demanded a £3 fee. They pleaded with him but he was adamant — no money, no marriage. Bridget, with a glint in her eye, left the church and said that she would raise the money.

True to her word she returned in half-an-hour with the money and the ceremony was completed to the satisfaction of all.

'Are we married now, right and proper? ' Bridget asked the priest.

'You are,' replied the priest, 'neither I nor anyone else can pull you asunder now.'

'Good,' said Bridget, 'there's the ticket for your hat and umbrella. I picked them up in the vestry and pawned them.'

****

Pat and Bridget, happily married, were walking home from the annual mission where they had just listened to a hell fire sermon on company keeping and married life.

'He had a lot to say on sexual relations, Pat,' said Bridget. 'Tell me, do we have any sexual relations?'

'Of course we do, woman,' said Pat.

'Well how is it that we never hear from them, not even a card at Christmas?'

****

'Every Irishman,' said Pat, 'should be married. After all there are many things you can't blame on the Government.'

****

14

After an uneventful twenty year courtship Bridget finally decided to speak up.

'Pat,' she said, 'don't you think it's time we were getting married? '

'Don't be a fool woman,' said Pat 'shure who would marry either of us at this stage of our lives? '

****

'I suppose Bridget that you carry a momento of some kind in that locket of yours?'

'Indeed I do, it's a lock of Pat's hair.'

'But your husband Pat is still alive.'

'Yes, but his hair is all gone.'

****

Pat and Bridget, whose married life was not without its difficulties, were receiving a lecture from their parish priest about their terrible quarrels.

'Why,' he said, 'your dog and cat would agree better than you do.'

'If your reverence will tie them together,' said Pat, 'you'll soon change your mind.'

****

'I'll never understand,' said Bridget, 'why a fine-looking lad like your brother Mick, would marry an ugly widow thirty years his senior.'

'When you want banknotes,' said Pat, 'you don't complain about their appearance or dates.'

****

An engagement is hardly a serious one that has not been broken off at least once.

Oscar Wilde.

****

Pat and Bridget have just celebrated their tin anniversary — twelve years of eating out of cans.

15

Give the woman in the bed more porter,
Give the man beside her water.

Old Irish Proverb.

****

Having popped the question to Bridget, Pat decided to question the pop by asking for his daughter's hand in marriage.
'Would you marry Bridget if she didn't have a penny to her name? ' Bridget's father asked.
'I would, sir,' said Pat eagerly.
'Then away with you,' said Bridget's father, 'we have enough fools in the family already.'

****

'My wife Mary,' a friend confided in Pat, 'is an angel.'
'You're lucky,' Pat told him, 'my wife Bridget is still alive.'

****

Pat took Bridget out in his car and became quite passionate.
'Bridget,' he said, 'get into the back.'
'No, I won't,' said Bridget.
'Why won't you get into the back of the car?' asked Pat.
'I'd prefer to stay in the front with you Pat,' said Bridget.

****

Pat went into a bookshop and asked a salesgirl if she had a book entitled *How to Master your Wife.*
'Our fiction section is upstairs, sir,' she told him.

****

Pat's wife Bridget took ill and was pronounced dead by the doctor. But as they were carrying her downstairs the coffin hit against the rail and Bridget sat up. She recovered fully and lived for twenty more years. Then she was taken ill and again pronounced dead. As the undertaker and his assistant were carrying the coffin down the narrow stairway, Pat called out, 'carefully, lads, carefully.'

****

One night there was a gas explosion and Pat and Bridget were sent through the roof and a hundred feet into the air in their double bed. Bridget, however, was not as upset as she might have been. It was the first time in twenty-five years that they had been out together.

****

When a woman makes a bad marriage she burns her coal but does not warm herself, says an old Irish proverb.

****

As Pat lay dying he noticed that there was a lovely aroma of roast beef coming from the kitchen.
'Bridget,' he called, 'weak as I am, I would love a few slices of that roast beef.'
'No,' said Bridget, 'there wouldn't be enough for the wake if I gave you any.'

****

Pat and Bridget's little boy came across some difficult words in his home exercise.
'What's a monologue, dad?' he asked Pat.
'A monologue son,' said Pat, 'is a conversation between a married man and his wife.'

****

Dear Bridget (Pat wrote),

Words cannot express how sorry I am that I broke off our engagement. I miss you so much and cannot live without you — can we not start all over again?

Your loving Pat.

P.S. Congratulations on winning £200,000 in the sweepstake.

****

'So your daughter Bridget finally got married,' a neighbour remarked to Bridget's father. 'It must be very hard to part with a beautiful daughter.'

'Yes,' said Bridget's father, 'but it's even harder to part with an ugly one.'

****

The parish priest met Bridget and said that he had heard that she was keeping company with a man despite the fact that her husband Pat had been dead only six months.

'That's true father,' said Bridget.

'And couldn't you have more respect for his memory? ' he continued.

'Ah father,' she smiled, 'you can't take memory in your arms on a cold night.'

****

Pat, a widower of eighty, proposed to Bridget, a widow of seventy-five, but she turned him down because he refused to let her three children come and live with them.

'I couldn't turn three poor children out into the cold hard world to fend for themselves,' she sobbed, 'and the youngest only fifty-three.'

****

One evening Pat and Bridget were sitting quietly in her father's sittingroom when Bridget decided to encourage him by switching off the light. Pat took the hint and went home.

****

Pat:	'Could I have your daughter Bridget's hand in marriage sir? '
Bridget's father:	'Certainly young man, I'm delighted to welcome you into the family.'
Pat:	'There's just one further thing sir.'
Bridget's father:	'What's that?'
Pat:	'Could I possibly borrow five pounds until the weekend sir?'
Bridget's father:	'Certainly not. I hardly know you.'

Bridget lay in bed on the first night of their honeymoon while Pat sat fully clothed on an armchair in the bedroom.
'Why don't you come to bed?' Bridget asked him.
'My mother told me that this would be the most exciting night of my life,' said Pat, 'and I don't want to miss any of it by going to sleep.'

****

Don't marry any woman under twenty; she is not come to her wickedness before that time; nor any woman who has a red nose at any age; because people make observations as you go along the street. 'A cast of the eye' – as the lady casts it on you – may pass muster under some circumstances; and I have even known those who thought it desirable; but absolute squinting is a monopoly of vision which ought not to be tolerated.

William Maginn.

****

Pat and Bridget were getting married but Pat wasn't too sure what fee he should pay the priest.
'There is no fixed fee,' said the priest, 'just pay me whatever you feel it's worth to have Bridget as your wife.'
Pat had a quick look at Bridget and handed the priest £1. The priest looked disgustedly at the money, then looked at Bridget, and gave Pat back seventy-five pence.

****

'Name even one thing,' said Pat in the course of a heated argument with Bridget, 'in which you will admit that my family scores over your family.'
'Your in-laws are better than my in-laws,' said Bridget.

****

Pat was asked why he had married for the fourth time.
'Marriage is a gamble,' he replied, 'and I'm a compulsive gambler.'

****

Pat called at the priests' presbytery and demanded to see the parish priest.

'I have a little problem in theology,' Pat told the parish priest, 'I want to know if it is right to profit financially from the mistakes of other people.'

'Certainly not,' said the parish priest, 'I'm quite definite on that point.'

'In that case,' said Pat, 'how about returning the money I paid you for marrying me to Bridget last month.'

****

Female murderers who have been sentenced to death get sheaves of offers of marriage.

George Bernard Shaw.

****

Bridget was standing at the bus stop when she noticed that the woman in front of her in the queue had earlobes over a foot long. Overcome with curiosity, Bridget asked her why her earlobes were in that condition.

'Well,' admitted the woman, 'it's because of my husband. When we go to bed at night, he likes to nibble my ear.'

'Well so does my husband Pat,' said Bridget, 'but I don't have earlobes over a foot long.'

'Ah yes,' said the woman, 'but you don't sleep in twin beds.'

****

Pat: 'I'm thinking of asking some girl to marry me, Bridget. What do you think of the idea?'

Bridget: 'I think it's a very good idea Pat, if you ask me.'

****

Bridget and Pat had just got engaged after a twenty year courtship.

'Pat,' said Bridget, 'I think there's a little flaw in the diamond of the engagement ring you bought me.'

'I thought you wouldn't see that,' said Pat, 'I thought love is blind.'

'Not stone blind,' said Bridget.

'Will you marry me?' Pat asked Bridget.
'Yes,' said Bridget simply.
Silence reigned for a few minutes.
'Is that all you have to say?' asked Bridget.
'I think I've said enough already,' said Pat.

****

Pat was fumbling in his pockets at the altar during his marriage to Bridget.
'What's the matter man,' said the priest irritably, 'have you lost the ring?'
'No, said Pat, 'but I've lost my enthusiasm.'

****

The phone rang in the maternity hospital and an excited voice at the other end of the line said.'
'Send an ambulance quickly, my wife Bridget is about to have a baby?'
'Calm down,' replied the nurse, 'tell me, is this her first baby?'
'No, said Pat, 'this is her husband Pat speaking.'

****

Bridget had twenty children.
'You must love children a lot,' a friend remarked.
'Love them?' said Bridget, 'I don't even know half of them.'

****

It was a wet stormy day when Pat buried his wife Bridget. Just as the funeral party left the graveyard there was a bright flash of lightning and a loud rumble of thunder. Pat looked up at the sky and commented:
'She's arrived up there already.'

****

Bridget's father: 'The man that marries my daughter Bridget will indeed be getting a prize.'
Pat: 'Could I possibly have a look at it first sir?'

21

Bridget's sister Mary was two-thirds married. She was there, the priest was there, but the groom didn't show up.

****

Pat (handing over a bunch of flowers to an amazed Bridget)
'Now don't get too excited — somebody left them behind him on the bus.

****

Pat looked out the window and called to Bridget:-
'Come quickly, there goes the woman that John Smith is in love with.'
Bridget dropped the dishes she was drying over the sink, knocked over a chair, and rushed to the window.
'You fool,' she said, 'that's his wife.'
'Of course it is,' smiled Pat.

****

Bridget was expecting her seventeenth child so she felt the time had come to break the news to her husband Pat.
'Pat,' she told him, 'the stork is about to pay us a visit.'
'Visit?' gasped Pat, 'why he practically lives here! '

****

Love is a temporary insanity curable by marriage.
Old Irish Proverb.

****

Bridget's little girl Mary was questioning her mother.
'God gives us our daily bread mother, doesn't He? '
Bridget: 'Yes dear.'
'And Santa Claus brings us presents at Christmas? '
'Yes dear.'
'And the stork brings us babies? '
'Yes dear.'
'Mother, why do we have father in the house at all? '

****

22

Nothing spoils a romance so much as a sense of humour in the woman.

Oscar Wilde.

****

Pat had been a T.D. for years and was hoping to be re-elected. In the middle of an important election speech, however, news was brought that his wife Bridget had just given birth to triplets. 'Triplets? ' he shouted from the platform, 'I don't believe it. I demand a recount.'

****

During their twenty-year courtship Pat and Bridget were out driving one evening.
'Would you like to see where I had my operation? ' asked Bridget.
'Yes,' said Pat excitedly.
'Well,' said Bridget, 'there's the hospital about fifty yards ahead on your side of the road.'

****

When Pat died, Bridget went to a draper's shop to buy him a shroud. Being a practical woman the first question she asked was the price.
'The cost is £5, madam,' said the draper.
'But I can get one down the street for £4,' protested Bridget.
'Those ones are no good, madam,' said the draper, 'the corpse would have his knees through it in a week.'

****

Bridget decided to try a mudpack as a beauty treatment. Pat said that she looked fine for a few days but then the mudpack wore off.

****

Butter to butter is no relish (An old Irish proverb quoted when men dance together, or two women kiss each other).
****

Definition of an Irish husband: He hasn't kissed his wife for twenty years but he will kill any man who does.

Pat was proposing to Bridget.

'I'm not a rich man,' he told her, 'but I will be soon – I'm my wealthy uncle's sole heir. He's a very old man and so ill that he can't live more than a few months.'

A few weeks later Bridget became his aunt.

****

'If you won't marry me,' said Pat to Bridget in desperation, 'I'll hang myself on the tree in front of your house.'

'Don't do that, for goodness sake,' said Bridget, 'you know my parents don't like you hanging about the house.'

****

A friend of Pat's called into the pub to give him an urgent message.

'You're wanted at home,' he told him, 'Bridget has just presented you with another rebate off your income tax.'

****

Bridget compared her husband Pat to an oil lamp because he was unsteady on his legs at times and, when half oiled inclined to explode, flared up occasionally, out at bed-time and smoked too much.

****

For twenty years Pat and Bridget were blissfully happy. Then they met.

****

'Come, come,' said Tom's father.   'At your time of life,
There's no longer excuse for thus playing the rake.
It is time you should think boy, of taking a wife.
'Why so it is, father – whose wife shall I take?'

Thomas Moore.

****

'Love,' said Pat, 'is the delusion that one woman differs from another.'

24

'My boy friend Pat is the meanest man in the world,' Bridget said to a friend.

'Why do you think that?' asked the friend.

'Well,' said Bridget, 'I've decided to refuse him if he proposes to me, and the mean old so-and-so won't propose.'

****

Pat was brought to court and charged with burglary and his wife Bridget was being cross-examined by an eminent lawyer.

'Did you know that this man was a burglar when you married him?' the lawyer asked her.

'I did,' replied Bridget.

'Then why on earth did you marry him?' persisted the lawyer.

'Well, said Bridget, 'I was getting on a bit and didn't want to be left on the shelf. I had the choice between a burglar and a lawyer so I married the burglar.'

'No further questions,' said the lawyer.

****

The three most incomprehensible things in the world are the labour of the bees, the ebb and flow of the tide, and the mind of woman.

Old Irish Proverb.

****

Before Pat met Bridget he took the desperate step of placing an advertisement in the matrimonial columns of a newspaper. It ran as follows:-

MATRIMONY

Eligible bachelor wishes to meet girl 18 — 45 with a view to the above. Must own her own tractor. Please send recent photograph (of tractor).

****

'He was a good husband to me,' sobbed Bridget after Pat had died, 'he always hit me with the soft end of the mop.'

****

'Do you dream about me, Pat?' asked Bridget.
'Shure, I can't sleep with dreaming of you darling,' answered Pat.

****

Pat proposed but Bridget refused him point blank.
'Why, Bridget, why?' he exclaimed.
'If you must know Pat,' she replied, 'It's because I'm a lesbian.'
'But that's no problem, girl', beamed Pat, 'you can go to your church and I'll go to mine.'

****

After ten years of marriage to Bridget, Pat sent the following letter to a bookshop:-

Dear Sir,

   Under separate cover I am sending back the book entitled *How to Control your Wife* which I bought from you a week ago. Unfortunately my wife Bridget will not let me keep it.

****

There are three kinds of woman a man cannot understand — a young woman, a middle-aged woman, and an old woman.

Old Irish Proverb.

****

Pat's little boy Mick was being examined in Christian Doctrine by the bishop and the parish priest to see if he was worthy to have the Sacrament of Confirmation conferred upon him.
'Tell me little man,' said the Bishop, 'what has the Catechism to say on the subject of Holy Matrimony?'
'Holy Matrimony,' said the little lad, 'is a place or state of punishment where some souls suffer for a time before going to Heaven.'
'You little fool,' shouted the parish priest, 'that's the answer for Purgatory'.
'Leave the little lad alone,' said the bishop, 'for all we know he may be telling the truth.'

****

When Pat died, sad to relate, he went to Hell. But within a few weeks he had made such a nuisance of himself down there that the Devil considered throwing him out.

'Look,' he told Pat, 'you're behaving as if you owned the place.'

'Why wouldn't I? ' said Pat, 'Bridget gave it to me before I died.'

****

Bridget had joined the Women's Liberation Movement so when Pat proposed she accepted on one condition.

'What's that, my treasure?' asked Pat.

'I can never agree to the word "obey" in the marriage ceremony,' she told him.

'Oh, don't worry about that,' said Pat, 'it won't make a bit of difference as long as you do what you are told after we are married.'

****

'Women,' claimed Pat, 'are mighty similar in one way — there's no two of them alike.'

****

Pat's friend Joe was taking a night course in Adult Education.

'Who is Jimmy Carter?' he asked Pat.

'I don't know,' said Pat.

'He's the President of The United States,' said Joe, 'you see, you should go to night school like I do. Now, do you know who Harold Wilson is?'

'No,' said Pat.

'He's the ex-Prime Minister of Britain,' said Joe, 'You see you should go to night school like I do.'

'Now I have a question for you,' said Pat, 'do you know who Micky O'Sullivan is?' 'I don't,' admitted Joe.

'He's the fellow who visits your wife every night when you're at night school,' smiled Pat.

****

Bridget: 'I've been trying to figure out where my husband Pat spends his evenings. Last night I came home early and there he was.'

****

Men have a much better time of it than women — they marry later and die earlier.

****

'When a lady is asked for a kiss,' said Pat, 'and says "no", she means "maybe"; if she says "maybe" she means "yes"; and if she says "yes" she is no lady.'

****

Pat and Bridget went through a new form of marriage ceremony where the couple are called to the altar by the priest after mass.
'Will those wishing to be married kindly come forward,' shouted the priest.
Pat, Bridget and about a dozen middle-aged spinsters stepped forward.

****

A man's first love is only a little foolishness and a lot of curiosity.
No self-respecting woman would take advantage of it.

George Bernard Shaw.

****

Shopkeeper: 'What sort of a toothbrush do you want sir? '
Pat: 'Give me a big strong one — there's ten kids in the family.'

****

'What proof have you that you can support my daughter? ' Bridget's father asked Pat.
Pat: 'Haven't I been engaged to her for over a year?'

****

Bridget: 'Darling, darling.'
Pat: 'Yes my love what is it?'
Bridget: 'Don't be silly, I was calling the dog.'

****

Pat and Bridget got married and about a year later a little stranger arrived to live with them. It was Bridget's uncle — he was a midget.

Bridget's Father: 'Do you think you could support my daughter if you married her?'
Pat: 'Yes sir.'
Bridget's Father: 'Have you ever seen her eat?'
Pat: 'Yes sir.'
Bridget's Father: 'Have you ever seen her eat when there's nobody looking?'

****

'Don't divorce your wife,' said Pat, 'buy her two dozen roses instead. The shock will kill her and you can use the roses for the funeral.'

****

'I'm looking for a husband,' said Bridget to a friend.
'But I thought you married Pat,' said the friend.
'Yes,' said Bridget, 'that's the husband I'm looking for!'

****

The Superintendant at the Asylum for the Insane received a telephone call from Pat asking him if any of his male inmates had escaped.
'No,' he replied, 'but why do you ask?'
'Somebody has just run off with my wife Bridget,' said Pat.

****

Bridget's little boy had been out playing.
'What game were you playing, my love?' she asked him.
'Postman', he replied.
'But how could you play postman if you had no letters? 'she asked.
'Oh, I had letters mummy,' he told her, 'I found a big packet of letters in your old trunk upstairs with a pink ribbon tied around them, so I put one under every door in the street.'

****

Pat was speaking on the telephone.
'Hello, Bridget, do you still love me?'
'This is not Bridget, it's Mary.'
'Sorry,' said Pat, 'I keep thinking it's Wednesday.'

****

'A kiss is a funny thing,' said Pat, 'It's of no use to one person, but fine for two. The small boy gets it for nothing, the young man has to ask for it, and the old man has to buy it. It's the baby's right, the lovers' privilege, and the hypocrite's mask. To the young girl it's faith; to the married woman, hope; and to the old maid, charity.'

****

'Where did you learn to kiss like that?' Bridget asked Pat when she had recovered her breath.
'I used to syphon petrol during the war,' said Pat.

****

Before she married Pat, Bridget had been asked to get married many times, but always by her father and mother.

****

Pat and Bridget were eloping.
'Be careful not to make any noise,' he told her, 'or you will wake your father.'
'No I won't,' said Bridget, 'he's holding the ladder.'

****

Pat and Bridget had to postpone their wedding because the tailor failed to deliver Pat's trousers on time. They sued him for promise of breeches.

****

A friend told Pat that he had bad luck with both of his wives. The first one ran away with another man and the second one didn't.

****

Bridget was hinting to Pat that he should buy her a new dress. 'I think I'd look good in something long and flowing,' she told him.
So he threw her into a river.

****

'What sort of stone would you like me to put on her grave?' the undertaker asked Pat after Bridget had passed away.
'Just make it a heavy one,' said Pat.

****

Pat went to the butchers to buy some meat.
'Is this steak tender?' he asked the assistant.
'It's as tender as your wife's heart,' said the assistant.
'I think I'll have a few lamb chops instead,' said Pat.

****

Forty years of romance make a woman look like a ruin —
Forty years of marriage make her look like a public building.

Oscar Wilde.

****

The ideal marriage, agreed Pat and Bridget, would be a deaf husband married to a blind wife.

****

Pat was quizzing Bridget about certain rumours that he had heard about her behaviour before they had met.

'Out with it woman,' he cried, 'is it true that you once had a baby out of wedlock?'

'Yes,' said Bridget, 'but it was only a little one.'

****

Bridget was so pestered by Pat's proposals that she finally married him to get rid of him.

****

Venus, a beautiful good-natured lady, was the goddess of love; Juno, a terrible shrew, the goddess of marriage; and they were always mortal enemies.

George Bernard Shaw

****

Bridget was getting on a bit and her marriage prospects seemed to be getting slimmer.

'Oh Lord,' she prayed one night, 'I'm not asking anything for myself, but please send my mother a son-in-law.'

****

'Those are Pat's ashes on the mantelpiece,' Bridget told a friend.

'I'm sorry to hear he has passed away,' said the friend.

'Oh he hasn't passed away,' said Bridget, 'he's just too lazy to find an ashtray.'

****

Pat's Uncle Tom had been married three times and all of his wives had died.

'Which marriage was the happiest?' Pat asked him.

'You bite three lemons,' retorted Uncle Tom, 'and tell me which was the sweetest.'

****

32

Pat was making an appointment at the dentist's.
'It will be £4 with gas,' said the dentist, 'but only £3 without gas.'
'I'll take the one costing £3,' said Pat.
'You're a brave man,' said the dentist, 'it's very painful without gas.'
'Oh, the appointment is not for me,' said Pat, 'it's for Bridget.'

****

Pat and his friend Mick, both now in their eighties were sitting on a park bench when a beautiful blond in her early twenties passed by.
'If only we were twenty years younger,' sighed Mick.
'Yes,' said Pat, 'we could run after her and steal her handbag.'

****

Definition of an Irish gentleman — One who never strikes a lady without provocation.

****

No man is a match for a woman except with a poker and a pair of hobnailed boots.

George Bernard Shaw.

****

'How are you getting on with your wife Bridget? ' Pat was asked.
'Well,' he replied, 'sometimes she's better and sometimes she's worse. But from the way she carries on when she's better, I think she's better when she is worse.'

****

Pat was asked by his parish priest to prove from the Scriptures that it is not lawful for a man to have more than one wife.
Pat quoted the verse: 'No man can serve two masters.'

****

Sing us the song you sang at your father's wedding.

Old Irish exhortation.

****

When Pat and Bridget finally got married he was 85 and she was 83. They spent the whole honeymoon trying to get out of the car.

****

Bridget arrived home wearing a new hat.
'Don't be alarmed,' she told Pat, 'it didn't cost me a penny. It was reduced from £20 to £10 so I bought it with the £10 I saved.'

****

Marriage will always be a popular institution, because it combines a maximum of temptation with a maximum of opportunity.

George Bernard S

****

Pat was a born optimist. Every year he called to the registry office to see if his marriage licence had expired.

****

Bridget came home from a Women's Liberation meeting and told her husband Pat that the meeting had been about free love.
'Surely you don't believe in free love, Bridget?' asked Pat in a shocked tone.
'Look,' said Bridget, 'have I ever sent you a bill?'

****

'Mother,' Bridget's little girl asked her, 'why does a bride always wear white on her wedding day? '
'White is the symbol of joy,' Bridget told her, 'so the bride wears white to show it's the happiest day of her life.'
'Why does the groom always wear black?' asked the little girl.

Pat and Bridget finally got married. It seems that Bridget put on so much weight that they couldn't get the engagement ring off her finger.

****

'Every man,' claimed Pat, 'should be married. If he gets a good wife, he'll be happy, and if he gets a bad wife, he'll become a philosopher.'

****

Lips that touch liquor will never touch my liquor.

Modern Irish Saying.

****

'Courtship,' said Bridget, 'is a time during which the girl decides whether she can do better or not.'

****

Pat died leaving his widow Bridget over twenty thousand pounds. The lawyers however, took months and months to settle the estate and Bridget was getting fed up with all the red tape and technicalities she had to wade through.
'Sometimes,' she confided in a friend, 'I'm sorry Pat ever died. Do you know I'd give five thousand of that money to have him back again.'

****

Pat and Bridget were about to be married, but Pat had been hearing rumours.
'Bridget,' he asked her bluntly, 'are you pregnant?'
'Yes Pat,' she replied, 'but only a little bit.'

****

'Pat and I never quarrel in front of the children,' said **Bridget** to a friend, 'we always send them outside to play first.'
'I've often noticed,' said the friend, 'that your kids have such lovely outdoor complexions.'

****

Cries Celia to a reverend dean,
'What reason can be given,
since marriage is a holy thing,
that there are none in heaven?'

'There are no women,' he replied;
She quick returns the jest;
'Women there are, but I'm afraid,
They cannot find a priest.'

John Winstanley (1678 — 1750).

****

Bridget went to the parish priest in an agitated condition.
'I want a separation from Pat,' she told him, 'I have reason to believe that he has been unfaithful to me.'
'What makes you think that?' asked the parish priest.
'I don't think he's the father of my last child,' said Bridget.

****

'Did you sleep with Bridget as the prosecution has alleged?' the judge asked Pat in a breach of promise case.
'Not a wink, your honour,' grinned Pat, 'not a wink! '

****

'A wife,' claimed Pat, 'is somebody who will share with you the troubles you wouldn't have had in the first place if you hadn't married her.'

Bridget was supporting an inebriated groom-to-be Pat at the altar rails when the priest said that he would not perform the ceremony.

'Take him away from here,' he told Bridget, 'and bring him back when he is sober.'

'But father,' sobbed Bridget, 'he won't come when he's sober.'

****

A match was made between Pat and Bridget, so they met for the first time on the day before the wedding. Pat was horrified to find that Bridget was lame, so he complained to his father who had made the match.

'Never mind,' said his father, clutching the dowry, 'sure it isn't for racing you want her.'

****

Pat was telling Bridget off because of the size of the household bills.

'Look at this gas bill,' he roared, 'you and your unsuccessful suicide attempts! '

****

Conversation was lively in the pub on the subject of who was the greatest man who ever lived. Some claimed it was Napoleon, others De Valera, while a third group supported Shakespeare.

'Gentlemen,' said Pat, 'the greatest man who ever lived was Francis Ignatius O'Brien.'

'Never heard of him,' said one fellow, 'where did you come across him? '

'I never met the man personally,' said Pat, 'but he was my wife Bridget's first husband.'

****

Pat was charged with deserting his wife Bridget.
'You have been found guilty,' said the judge, 'I award your wife twenty pounds a week.'
'That's very good of your honour,' said Pat, 'I'll try to give her a few quid myself! '

****

Pat went courting Bridget having spent hours preparing himself. Dressed in a blue suit, a yellow shirt, a green tie, and brown boots, he was seen off by his mother with a dash of holy water. About twenty minutes later he returned in a state of agitation and nervousness.
'Well,' said his mother, 'did you see Bridget?'
'I did, mother,' said Pat, 'and if I hadn't hidden behind a haystack, she would have seen me too.'

****

Pat, as always the shy lover, was out walking on his farm with his girlfriend Bridget. Suddenly they came upon two cattle rubbing noses.
'Bridget,' said Pat passionately, 'I'd love to do that.'
'What's stopping you,' said Bridget, 'they're your own cattle aren't they? '

****

The safety of women consists in one circumstance — men do not possess at the same time the knowledge of thirty-five and the blood of seventeen.

William Maginn (1793 — 1842)

****

Bridget decided to encourage her lover Pat a bit one evening, during their twenty-year courtship.
'Boo hoo,' she cried, 'nobody loves me and my hands are cold.'
'Don't worry,' responded Pat, 'your mother loves you and you can always sit on your hands.'

'Marriage,' claimed Pat, 'is a long meal, with the dessert served as first course.'

****

Bridget was walking to Mass, sporting a black eye.
'Who gave you the black eye, Bridget?' asked the Parish Priest.
'Pat,' said Bridget belligerently, 'and who better!'.

****

Pat and Bridget's marriage fell into two distinct phases. For the first ten years Bridget tried to correct the effects of the way that Pat's mother had brought him up. For the next ten years she pampered her own children in exactly the same way.

****

The custom of a father's 'giving away' his daughter when she is being married is still widely observed in Ireland.
(But not in the sense of 'several fellows in the congregation could have given Bridget away, but they kept quiet.')
Not so widely known however, are the following 'give-away' lines:
'Take her and when you've had her around the house as long as I've had her, you'll be sick and tired of her.'
and 'Here she is, and you can have her mother as well.'

****

Pat was so lazy he married Bridget, a widow with five children.

****

Pat and Bridget's marriage ran into trouble right from the start. They fell out about who should cut the wedding cake.

****

Pat decided to go to London for his honeymoon. However, he left Bridget behind because she had been to London before.

****

Pat and Bridget had just presented their seventeenth child for Baptism.
'I suppose,' said the priest with heavy sarcasm, 'that you will be back next year to have the eighteenth baptism? '
'Indeed, we will not,' said Pat, 'Bridget and I have just found out what's been causing them.'

****

Isadora Duncan is said to have proposed marriage to George Bernard Shaw. She claimed that with her beauty and his brains they would produce the perfect child. Shaw's reply was: 'But what if the unfortunate child were to inherit my beauty and your brains? '

****

After a whirlwind four year courtship, Pat finally proposed to Bridget.
'Pat,' she replied, 'what's the difference between me and a Jersey cow?'
'Faith, I don't know,' said Pat.
'Then,' said Bridget, 'why not marry the cow?'

****

Bridget had just presented Pat with their fourteenth child, so Pat's workmates decided to present him with a plaque to mark the occasion.
'Thanks a million fellows,' said Pat, 'but tell me one thing, why does it have a picture of a duck in the centre?'
'That's no duck,' they told him, 'that's a stork with his legs worn off.'

'What income do you have to support a family? ' Bridget's father asked Pat.

'About £2,000 a year,' said Pat.

'Good,' he replied, 'now with the £2,000 a year I'm planning to settle on her you should be able to live in reasonable comfort.'

'Excuse me sir,' said Pat, 'I was including that.'

****

A married woman commonly falls in love with a man as unlike her husband as is possible — but a widow very often marries a man extremely resembling the defunct. The reason is obvious.

William Maginn (1793 — 1842).

****

After only ten years of courtship Pat grabbed Bridget and kissed her passionately.

'Oh Pat,' she cried, 'how could you take such a liberty?' 'Now I'll have to tell the priest in confession that you kissed me passionately on two occasions.'

'What do you mean girl? said Pat, 'I only kissed you once.'

'But you're going to do it again, Pat, aren't you?' asked Bridget. anxiously.

****

Pat, who had worked for twenty years as the skipper of a boat, fell overboard and was drowned. After the funeral a friend of Bridget's asked the inevitable question —

'Did he leave you much?'

'He did indeed,' said Bridget, 'nearly twenty thousand pounds.'

'Isn't that wonderful,' said the friend, 'and him that couldn't read or write.'

'Or swim,' said Bridget.

****

Pat and Bridget had the quickest courtship ever. They met on Friday, got engaged on Saturday, and by Sunday he owed her £200.

Pat came home drunk every night so Bridget decided that something would have to be done. Knowing that he had to pass through a graveyard on his way home she hired a man to dress in a white sheet and jump in front of Pat from behind a tombstone.

'Boo,' he shouted, 'I'm the devil.'

'I'm pleased to meet you,' said Pat, 'I married your sister.'

****

One morning Pat received a letter in the post warning him 'If you don't send five thousand pounds to the above address immediately, we will kidnap your wife Bridget and you will never see her again.'

Pat sent the following reply:

Dear Sir,

I haven't got five thousand pounds, but your offer interests me greatly.

****

'Who is that very ugly woman over there in that dreadful hat?' Pat was asked by a man at a party.

'That's my wife Bridget,' said Pat.

'Pardon me,' said the man, 'my mistake.'

'No,' said Pat, 'my mistake.'

****

Bridget was attending her convent school reunion where the Reverend Mother was asking each of her ex-pupils what career she had chosen.

'I've become a prostitute,' said one, and the Reverend Mother promptly fainted.

When she was revived she asked the girl what she had said.

'A prostitute,' repeated the girl.

'Thank Heavens,' said the Reverend Mother, 'I thought for a moment you had said a Protestant.

****

Before Bridget met Pat she fell in love with a Jewish chap, but the parish priest told her that they couldn't marry unless he became a Catholic. So Bridget set to work on an intensive conversion course for over a month. One night however, she arrived at the priest's house in a tearful condition.
'What's the matter now?' asked the parish priest.
'I've overdone the conversion,' wailed Bridget, 'Now he wants to become a priest.'

****

Bridget was only a poteen maker's daughter but Pat loved her still.

****

Pat applied for a divorce on the grounds that Bridget's father didn't have a licence for the shotgun.

****

Bridget: 'Before we got married you told me you were well off.'
Pat: 'I was and I didn't know it.'

****

Pat and his grandfather were discussing the subject of marriage.
'Would you get married if you could live your life all over again?' Pat asked him.
'I would not,' he replied. 'In fact if they had electric blankets and sliced bread when I was a lad, I never would have married.'

****

Bridget: What's the best way to look after a wedding ring?
Pat: 'Dip it in dishwater three times a day.'

****

Pat: 'Would you say "Yes" if I asked you to marry me?'
Bridget: 'Would you ask me to marry you if I said I would say "Yes" if you asked me to marry you?'

43

Lord, I wonder what fool it was first invented kissing.

Jonathan Swift.

****

Pat had proposed to Bridget and was being interviewed by his prospective father-in-law.

'Do you think you are earning enough to support a family? he asked Pat.

'Yes sir,' replied Pat, 'I'm sure I am.'

'Think carefully now,' said Bridget's father, 'there are twelve of us.'

****

Marry a woman from the mountain and you marry the entire mountain.

Old Irish Proverb.

****

Pat's son became an actor and one evening rushed home to his father in a state of great excitement.

'Guess what, dad,' he announced, 'I've just been given my first part. I play a man who has been married for twenty five years.'

'Keep it up son,' said Pat, 'some day you may get a speaking part.'

****

Pat and Bridget's little five-year-old boy Billy was talking with the little boy next door.

'What age are you?' Billy asked him.

'I don't know,' the little fellow replied.

'Do women bother you?' asked Billy.

'No,' said the little fellow.

'Then you're four,' said Billy.

****

44

'My wife Bridget is very ill,' Pat told a friend.
'Is she dangerously ill?' the friend asked anxiously
'No,' said Pat, 'she's too ill to be dangerous.'

****

When Pat died Bridget was being consoled by an old friend of the family.
'I'll miss him terribly,' wailed Bridget.
'I know you will,' said the friend, 'but at least from now on you won't be wondering where he is at night!'

****

Bridget and Pat had just celebrated the twentieth anniversary of the beginning of their courtship.
'Bridget,' began Pat timidly, 'did you ever think of marrying?
'No,' said Bridget coyly, 'the subject never entered my head.'
'I'm sorry,' said Pat, 'for bringing the subject up.'
'Wait a minute Pat,' called Bridget, 'you've set me thinking.'

****

Pat and Bridget had just had their eighteenth child so Bridget went to the doctor and asked if he could give her a hearing aid.
'A hearing aid,' asked the doctor, 'how will that help you space your family more effectively?'
'Well,' explained Bridget, 'I'm a little deaf, so every night when we go to bed Pat says, "would you like to go to sleep or what?" and I always say, "what"

****

For Christmas Bridget gave Pat two ties, one red and the other green. On Christmas morning Pat came down to breakfast wearing the green tie.
'What's the matter with the red one then?' asked Bridget.

****

45

Pat and Bridget raised eighteen children all of whom got married but much to the old couple's disgust after ten years they were still waiting for a grandchild. Before their Christmas dinner, with the whole family around the table, Pat announced, 'I regret to say I don't see any grandchildren around this table of mine. I want you all to know that I will give ten thousand pounds to the first couple of you who present me with a grandchild. We will now say grace.'

When he raised his eyes again, he and Bridget were the only ones left at the table.

****

Pat and Bridget were having the father and mother of a row, and Bridget was on the receiving end of blow after blow. When Pat had knocked her down for about the twentieth time he found to his horror that the parish priest had entered the house by the back door and was observing the scene. Quick as a flash he shouted 'Now, Bridget will you go to Mass?'

****

Pat and Bridget were going on a continental holiday, but Bridget's passport was out of date.

'Can you prove that this woman is your wife?' the customs official asked.

'Look,' whispered Pat, 'I'll give you £25 if you can prove she isn't.'

****

Bridget had been killed in an accident and the police were questioning Pat.

'Did she say anything before she died?' they asked him.

'She spoke without interruption for about forty years,' said Pat.

****

Pat's wife Bridget died on a Sunday and he arranged the funeral for the following Sunday.
'We always promised we would have a quiet week together,' he explained.

****

Pat came home from work to find Bridget in a tearful condition.
'Boo hoo,' she cried, 'the dog has just eaten the dinner I cooked for you.'
'Don't worry,' Pat consoled her, 'I'll buy you another dog.'

****

'One woman kissing another,' said Pat, 'is like two boxers shaking hands before a fight.'

****

Pat was on the visiting committee of the local mental hospital and was being shown round by a young doctor.
'Here's a sad case,' said the doctor, 'see how he clutches that doll all the time.
He was engaged to a girl he loved very deeply, but at the last minute she jilted him and married another man.'
They passed along the corridor to the next cell which was heavily barred and thickly padded.
'And this,' said the doctor, 'is the man she married.'

****

'Women,' said Pat, 'are like elephants. Everybody likes to look at them but nobody likes to have to keep one.'

****

Pat had been killed in a brawl and the local parish priest was assigned to inform his wife Bridget of the tragedy. When he called, Bridget was finishing her dinner, a pig's crubeen. She continued eating as the parish priest unfolded the sad news. As the amazed parish priest waited for her reaction she told him.
'Hang on for a minute until I finish this crubeen, and then you'll hear crying and lamentation such as you've never heard before.'

47

Bridget was about to die so she asked Pat for a last request.
'At the funeral, Pat,' she begged, 'let my mother ride with you in the front coach.'
'All right,' said Pat, 'but it will ruin the day for me.'

****

After Pat died, Bridget visited a medium and successfully made contact with him.
'Are you happy now?' she asked him.
'Yes,' said Pat, 'I'm very happy.'
'Happier than you were, when you were with me? ' she asked.
'Yes,' said Pat, 'far happier than I was with you.'
'Heaven must be a lovely place Pat,' sighed Bridget wistfully.
'Who said anything about Heaven? ' said Pat.

****

A very nervous Pat was attempting to propose to Bridget.
'Bridget,' he said nervously, 'I'd like to ask you a question.'
'Yes Pat,' said Bridget wearily, 'what is it? '
'Do you think you could every marry a man like me? '
'Provided he wasn't too much like you,' said Bridget.

****

If you want praise – die, If you want blame – marry.

Old Irish Proverb.

****

Pat's young nephew Brian was going on his first date so he asked his uncle for advice.
'Should I kiss her unexpectedly,' Brian asked him, 'or should I build up to it ? '
'Look, boy,' smiled Pat, 'you can't kiss a girl unexpectedly, only sooner than she thought you would.'

48